Red Is the Color of My True Love's Neck

Jeff Foxworthy

With illustrations by David Boyd

RUTLEDGE HILL PRESS

Nashville, Tennessee

A Division of Thomas Nelson Publishers

Since 1798

www.thomasnelson.com

Published by Rutledge Hill Press, a Division of Thomas Nelson, Inc., P.O. Box 141000, Nashville, Tennessee 37214.

Rutledge Hill Press books may be purchased in bulk for educational, business, fundraising, or sales promotional use. For information, please e-mail SpecialMarkets@ThomasNelson.com.

Library of Congress Cataloging-in-Publication Data

Foxworthy, Jeff.
    Red is the color of my true love's neck / Jeff Foxworthy with illustrations by David Boyd.
        p. cm.
    ISBN 1-4016-0228-2 (tradepaper)
    1. Rednecks—Humor. I. Title.
PN6231.R38F684 2005
818'.5402—dc22   2005025925

Printed in the United States of America

06 07 08 09 — 5 4 3 2

Introduction

All my life I've heard the saying, "There's someone for everyone." No matter how ugly or ornery someone may be, there always seems to be at least one person who thinks they're cute.

My dad found that "someone" six different times. He liked *getting* married, but *staying* married gave him lots of trouble. One of his marriages failed because of religious differences—he thought he was God and she threatened to knock him to Kingdom Come.

The most common reason given for divorces today is "incompatibility." In my opinion, incompatibility is often the result of mixed marriages—rednecks marrying non-rednecks. So in order to promote healthier and happier relationships, I have compiled this guide to redneck compatibility.

For example, red is the color of your true love's neck if . . .

- The most romantic moment in your life was captured on a security camera.
- You've ever slow danced in a Waffle House.
- You think rug burns are a sexually transmitted disease.
- Your wedding reception was a tailgate party.

There are a bunch of clues to compatibility in this book. If you and your "special someone" recognize yourselves in at least a dozen or so, there's a good chance you're headed for redneck bliss. That's when a husband gives his wife a glue gun for their anniversary and she thinks it's a great gift.

So snuggle up in the recliner with someone special and enjoy this volume of redneck education. And don't be surprised if after a few minutes he whispers those three little words . . . "Pull my finger."

— Jeff Foxworthy

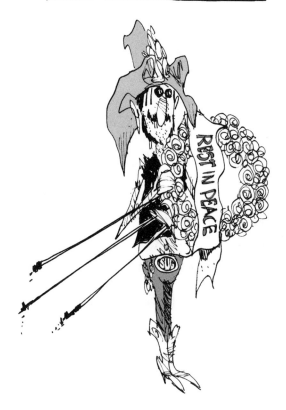

You've ever given your
date flowers you stole
from a cemetery.

You've ever french-
kissed within five feet
of a Dumpster.

You had your
anniversary dinner
at the food court
in the mall.

In preparation for a romantic evening, you stop by the grocery store for a bottle of Mr. Bubble.

You've ever hot-wired
a motel vibrating bed.

Sex education at
your school included
advice on avoiding
the steering wheel.

You have to roll up
your sleeve and look
at your arm to spell
your wife's name.

11

You've ever spray-painted your girlfriend's name on an overpass.

Your honeymoon hotel advertised "Truckers Welcome."

13

You're making "rabbit ears" behind the bride in your wedding photos.

You dated your
daddy's current wife
in high school.

15

Your wife puts candles on a pan of
corn bread for your birthday.

A dating service
matches you up
with a relative.

You said your wedding vows while watching a football game out of the corner of your eye.

You've ever accepted an invitation written on a bathroom wall.

19

Your favorite pickup
line is "Dang, are those
things real?!"

20

There were dogs in the church on
your wedding day.

Those three little
words you whisper to
your wife at night are
"Pull my finger."

You had a prom night
and a wedding night,
but not in that order.

You remember the entire NASCAR schedule, but can't remember your wife's birthday.

24

You honk your horn
during love scenes at
the drive-in.

You hope heaven is kind of like Hooters.

26

Your wife's jewelry box plays "Beast of Burden" when opened.

Taking your wife on a cruise means circling the Dairy Queen.

Your wedding invitations say, "Same time, same place."

For laughs, you watch
your wife's delivery
video backwards.

You think rug burns are a sexually transmitted disease.

31

Your current wife was a bridesmaid at your first wedding.

You've ever celebrated your wife's
birthday in a tree.

You view the upcoming family reunion as a chance to meet women.

Your will states your wife can't touch your money until she's 14.

35

When people talk about the Big
Easy, you think they are
referring to your ex-girlfriend.

You proposed to your
wife while working
under your truck.

37

Your definition
of "getting lucky"
is passing the
emissions test.

The last time you fought with your wife was on *The Jerry Springer Show.*

Your favorite sex position is
"awake."

You met your wife
through the personal
ads in *Bowhunter*
magazine.

You've been married three times and still have the same in-laws.

You think
hors d'oeuvres are
those girls at the
intersection downtown.

43

You're making payments
on more than one
wedding ring.

You've ever asked a widow
for her phone number
at the funeral home.

You refer to your van
as "the Love Machine."

46

The first time you saw your wife in lingerie, you had to pay a cover charge.

Winn-Dixie catered
your wedding.

Your mother genuinely admires
your girlfriend's tattoos.

You've ever had to move a baby seat to make love.

You think "dinner reservations" means they've tasted your wife's cooking.

You've ever had sex
in a satellite dish.

The fountain at your wedding spewed beer instead of champagne.

You can't remember what name you used on your marriage license.

You hit on
the midwife while
your wife's in labor.

You married your wife
for her socket set.

Your favorite cologne
is Deep Woods OFF.

You think "showing a girl a good time" means letting her bait the hook.

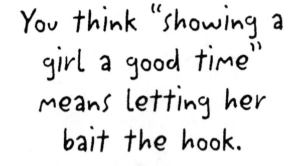

58

You gave your wife a glue gun for your anniversary.

59

Truckers tell your wife
to watch her language.

You had a marriage license before you had a driver's license.

61

You've ever told a bride, "You clean up pretty good."

Your prenuptial
agreement mentions
chickens.

63

You and your wife
stay married for the
sake of the dogs.

The most romantic moment
of your life was captured
on a security camera.

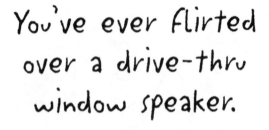

You've ever flirted over a drive-thru window speaker.

You had to take gum
out of your mouth to
kiss the bride.

Your wife would rather fish off a
bridge than shop for clothes.

You whistle at women
in church.

Any of your fantasies involve Wal-Mart.

You think
disposable diapers
are an appropriate
wedding gift.

Any of your children were conceived at a traffic signal.

You give your marital status as "often."

You think a sex change means trying the backseat.

Two of your weddings
made America's
Funniest Home Videos.

You took your
honeymoon photos to
show-and-tell.

You've ever lost your wife in a poker game.

You learned
the facts of life
by watching dogs.

Proposing to your wife included the words "when I get out."

You practice "safe sex" by putting
on the emergency brake.

You've ever
used lard in bed.

81

You've ever opened a
beer while making love.

The stripper at your bachelor party was your fiancée.

You've used food stamps
on a date.

84

You delayed your wedding
because of hunting season.

You taped WWF wrestling over your wedding video.

Your wife owns a camouflage nightie.

87

You think a Volvo is part of a
woman's anatomy.

Your wedding reception was a tailgate party.

89

Your wife sleeps on
the couch every time
you eat at Taco Bell.

You go to the
Laundromat to pick
up women.

Any of your wedding gifts came from an Army Navy store.

You and your wife
compare beer bellies.

You consider dating
second cousins to be
"playing the field."

You honeymooned in
the pop-up camper in
your parents' backyard.

You Might Be a Redneck If . . .

You've ever slow danced in a
Waffle House.